The Little Book of
# WRINKLIES' WIT
# & WISDOM

First published in Great Britain in 2008 by Prion

an imprint of the
Carlton Publishing Group
20 Mortimer Street
London W1T 3JW

4  6  8  10  9  7  5

Some of the material in this book was
previously published in *Wrinklies' Wit & Wisdom*

A catalogue record for this book is available from the British Library

ISBN 978-1-85375-652-8

Printed in China

The Little Book of

# WRINKLIES' WIT & WISDOM

Humorous Quotes
About Getting On a Bit

Rosemarie Jarski

PRION

Old is the new young! Grey is the new black! Saga-louts are the new lager-louts! This sparkling collection of wrinklies' wit and wisdom explodes the old stereotypes of knitting grannies and doddering grandpas. Today's golden girls and silver studs are more likely to take inspiration from age-defying stars like Joan Collins, Bruce Forsyth and Mick Jagger: they're growing old disgracefully, living life to the full, taking on new challenges and keeping a sense of humour. If laughter is the best medicine, consider this your prescription for a long and happy life. You see, he who laughs, lasts.

The secret of staying young
is to live honestly, eat slowly,
and lie about your age.

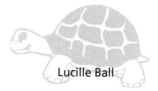

Lucille Ball

I'm very pleased to be here.
Let's face it, at my age I'm
pleased to be anywhere.

George Burns

How old would you be if you didn't know how old you were?

Satchel Paige

I'm 80, but in my own mind, my age veers. When I'm performing on stage, I'm 40; when I'm shopping in Waitrose, I'm 120.

Humphrey Lyttelton

He was either a man of about a 150 who was rather young for his years or a man of about a 110 who had been aged by trouble.

P. G. Wodehouse

I'm 42 around the chest, 52 around the waist, 92 around the golf course and a nuisance around the house.

Groucho Marx

I'm 52 years of age now, but I prefer to think of myself as 11 centigrade.

Tom Lehrer

Never trust a woman who
tells one her real age.
A woman who would tell
one that, would
tell anything.

Oscar Wilde

If you want to know how old a woman is, ask her sister-in-law.

Ed Howe

The years that a woman subtracts from her age are not lost. They are added to the ages of other women.

Diane de Poitiers

Age is a question of mind over matter. If you don't mind, age don't matter.

Satchel Paige

I recently turned 60.
Practically a third of my
life is over.

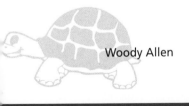

Woody Allen

Here I sit, alone and 60,
bald and fat and full of sin;
cold the seat and loud the cistern,
as I read the Harpic tin.

Alan Bennett

Eighty's a landmark and
people treat you differently
than they do when you're 79.
At 79, if you drop something
it just lies there. At 80, people
pick it up for you.

Helen Van Slyke

The three ages of man: youth, middle age, and "You're looking wonderful!"

Dore Schary

Two weeks ago we celebrated
my uncle's 103rd birthday.
One hundred and three
– isn't that something?
Unfortunately he wasn't
present. How could he be?
He died when he was 29.

**Victor Borge**

Growing old is like being increasingly penalized for a crime you haven't committed.

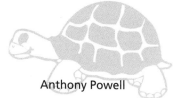

**Anthony Powell**

— You know what the worst
part about getting old is?
— Your face?

Blanche Devereaux and

Dorothy Zbornak,

*The Golden Girls*

You know you're getting old
when you feel like the day
after the night before and you
haven't even been anywhere.

Milton Berl

You know you're getting old
when you go on holiday and
always pack a sweater.

Denis Norden

You know you're getting old when you're dashing through Marks and Spencer's, spot a pair of Dr Scholl's sandals, stop, and think, hmm, they look comfy.

Victoria Wood

An uncle of mine, a retired headmaster, said that the first time he felt old was when he was in a queue at his local post office to collect his old age pension and found himself behind a former pupil who was there for the same purpose.

Paul Kelvin-Smith

At a church social, a little boy came up and asked me how old I was. I said, "I'm 76." "And you're still alive?" he said.

Jack Wilson

Old age is not for sissies.

Bette Davis

One day, aged 45, I just went into the kitchen to make myself a cup of tea, and when I came out I found I was 68.

Thora Hird

Old age is like underwear.
It creeps up on you.

Lois L. Kaufman

To me, old age is always 15 years older than I am.

Bernard Baruch

I don't feel old. In fact I don't feel anything until noon. Then it's time for my nap.

Bob Hope

Old is when your wife says,
"Let's go upstairs and make
love," and you answer,
"Honey, I can't do both."

**Red Buttons**

I swear I'm ageing about as well as a beach-party movie.

Harvey Fierstein, *Torch Song Trilogy*

I said to my husband,
my boobs have gone,
my stomach's gone, say
something nice about my legs.
He said, "Blue goes
with everything."

Joan Rivers

After 40 a woman has to
choose between losing her
figure or her face. My advice
is to keep your face and stay
sitting down.

Barbara Cartland

I don't have a beer belly. It's a Burgundy belly and it cost me a lot of money.

**Charles Clarke**

Mick Jagger told me the wrinkles on his face were laughter lines, but nothing is that funny.

George Melly

Dorothy, was Sophia naked just now or does her dress really need ironing?

Rose Nylund, *The Golden Girls*

Moisturisers do work. The rest is pap. There is nothing on God's earth that will take away 30 years of arguing with your husband.

Anita Roddick

Wrinkle cream doesn't work. I've been using it for two years and my balls still look like raisins.

Harland Williams

Like all ruins, I look best by moonlight. Give me a sprig of ivy and an owl under my arm and Tintern Abbey would not be in it with me.

W. S. Gilbert

The easiest way to diminish
the appearance of wrinkles is
to keep your glasses off when
you look in the mirror.

Joan Rivers

The secret of my youthful appearance is simply – mashed swede. As a face-mask, as a night-cap and, in an emergency, as a draught-excluder.

*Kitty*, Victoria Wood

When it comes to staying young, a mind-lift beats a face-lift any day.

Marty Bucella

Caesar had his toga,
Adam had his leaf, but when
I wear a thong it gives my
piles such grief.

Sandra Mayhew

— Now, if you'll excuse me, I'm going to slip into something that will make me look my best.
— May I suggest a time-machine?

Blanche Devereaux and
Sophia Petrillo, *The Golden Girls*

A wonderful woman
my grandmother – 86 years
old and not a single grey
hair on her head. She's
completely bald.

Les Dawson

I knew I was going bald when it was taking longer and longer to wash my face.

Harry Hill

People ask me how long it takes to do my hair. I don't know, I'm never there.

Dolly Parton

I'm at the age when food has taken the place of sex in my life. In fact, I've just had a mirror put over my kitchen table.

Rodney Dangerfield

Gin is a dangerous drink. It's clear and innocuous-looking. You also have to be 45, female and sitting on the stairs.

Dylan Moran

Why is it all the things I like eating have been proven to cause tumours in white mice?

Robert Benchley

You do live longer with bran,
but you spend the last
15 years on the toilet.

Alan King

I don't eat health foods.
At my age I need all the
preservative I can get.

George Burns

You gotta stay in shape. My grandmother started walking five miles a day when she was 60. She's 97 today and we don't know where the hell she is.

Ellen DeGeneres

I keep fit. Every morning, I do a 100 laps of an Olympic-sized swimming pool—in a small motor launch.

Peter Cook

Whenever I get the urge to exercise, I lie down until the feeling passes away.

Robert M. Hutchins

The Rolling Stones are on tour again. They were gonna call the tour, "Hey! You! Get Offa My Stairlift!"

David Letterman

The ageing process has you
firmly in its grasp if
you never get the urge to
throw a snowball.

Doug Larson

Whatever a man's age, he
can reduce it several years
by putting a bright-coloured
flower in his buttonhole.

Mark Twain

My Nan, God bless 'er, gets things a bit mixed up. She said to me the other day, "I've bought one of those new George Formby grills."

Peter Kay

— Barbara, didn't Elsie next
  door have implants?
— No, eggplants Mam.

Nana and Barbara Royle,
*The Royle Family*

I don't want to end up in an old folks' home wearing incompetence pads. I'm still compost mentis.

Harriet Wyn

As you grow old, you lose interest in sex, your friends drift away and your children often ignore you. There are other advantages, of course, but these are the outstanding ones.

Richard Needham

One of the delights of being a senior citizen is it's easy to annoy young people. Step one: get in the car. Step two: turn the indicator on. Step three: leave it on for 50 miles.

David Letterman

My kitchen linoleum is so black and shiny that I waltz while I wait for the kettle to boil. This pleasure is for the old who live alone.

Florida Scott-Maxwell

One of the delights known to age, and beyond the grasp of youth, is that of Not Going.

J. B. Priestley

At the age of 80, there are
very few pleasures left to
me, but one of them is
passive smoking.

Baroness Trumpington

If you resolve to give up
smoking, drinking and loving,
you don't actually live longer
– it just seems longer.

Clement Freud

I was brought up to respect my elders and now I'm 87 I don't have to respect anybody.

George Burn

At 76, there is nothing nicer than nodding off while reading, going fast asleep then being woken up by the crash of the book on the floor, then saying to myself, well it doesn't matter much. An admirable feeling.

A. J. P. Taylor

One of the advantages of being
70 is that you need
only four hours' sleep. True,
you need it four times a day,
but still.

Denis Norden

By the time you're 80 years old you've learned everything. You only have to remember it.

George Burns

The only reason I wear glasses is for little things, like driving my car – or finding it.

Woody Allen

My grandmother is over 80 and still doesn't need glasses. Drinks right out of the bottle.

Henny Youngman

Sometimes it's fun to sit
in your garden and try to
remember your dog's name.

Steve Martin

— Mother, are you still on the computer?
— Yes, dear. Sometimes you get into a porn loop and just can't get out.

Edina Monsoon and Mum,
*Absolutely Fabulous*

The older you get, the better you get – unless you're a banana.

Anon

One positive thing about getting older is that you develop a sense of perspective about your legacy to future generations. People say things like, "We're going to use up our Earth's resources. The Earth will be uninhabitable by 2050." And I find myself nodding and going, "No problem, I'll be dead."

Dave Barry

— You're now 76 years old. Do you have any regrets in life?
— Yes, I haven't had enough sex.

Interviewer and John Betjeman

My greatest regret is not knowing at 30 what I knew about women at 60.

Arthur Miller

If I had my life to live over again, I'd make the same mistakes – only sooner.

Tallulah Bankhead

At age 20, we worry about what others think of us; at 40, we don't care what they think of us; at 60, we discover they haven't been thinking of us at all.

Bob Hope

My grandma told me, "The good news is, after menopause the hair on your legs gets really thin and you don't have to shave any more. Which is great, because it means you have more time to work on your new moustache."

Karen Habe

I refuse to think of them as
chin hairs. I think of them as
stray eyebrows.

Janette Barbe

— How do you know which pills to take?
— Doesn't make any difference. Whatever they fix, I got.

Oscar Madison and Felix Ungar,
*The Odd Couple II*

Casey came home from seeing the doctor looking very worried. His wife said, "What's the problem?" He said, "The doctor told me I have to take a pill every day for the rest of my life." She said, "So what, lots of people have to take a pill every day for the rest of their lives." He said, "I know, but he only gave me four."

**Hal Roach**

I rang the Enema Helpline.
They were very rude.

Jack Dee

Always keep tubes of
haemorrhoid ointment and
Deep Heat rub well separated
in your bathroom cabinet.

P. Turner, top tip, *Viz*

My Granny wore a hearing aid that was always tuned too low, because when she turned it up, it whistled, and every dog in Dublin rushed to her side.

Terry Wogan

When I turn my hearing aid up to ten, I can hear a canary break wind six miles away.

Sophia Petrillo, *The Golden Girls*

Use your health, even to the point of wearing it out. That is what it is for. Spend all you have before you die; do not outlive yourself.

George Bernard Shaw

I took a physical for some life insurance. All they would give me was fire and theft.

Milton Berle

My wife and I took out life insurance policies on one another, so now it's just a waiting game.

Bill Dwyer

As you get older, you've probably noticed that you tend to forget things. You'll be talking at a party, and you'll *know* that you know this person, but no matter how hard you try, you can't remember his or her name. This can be very embarrassing, especially if he or she turns out to be your spouse.

**Dave Barry**

First, you forget names, then you forget faces. Next, you forget to pull your zipper up and finally you forget to pull it down.

Leo Rosenberg

The Mayoress was visiting an old folks' home. As she went round she saw an old lady sitting there and said to her, brightly, "Good morning." The old lady looked a bit puzzled, so the Mayoress said, "Do you know who I am?" The old lady gave her a sympathetic look and said, "No, dear, but if you ask the matron, she'll tell you."

Anon

— Do you remember
the minuet?
— Dahling, I can't
even remember the men
I *slept* with!

Interviewer and Tallulah Bankhead

They tell you that you'll lose your mind when you grow older. What they don't tell you is that you won't miss it very much.

Malcolm Cowley

People say, oh, it's not like the good old days. When were the good old days? In 1900 your doctor was also your barber. "Say, will you take a little off the sides when you take out my spleen?"

Joe Ditzel

In my day, a juvenile delinquent was a kid who owed tuppence on an overdue library book.

Max Bygrave

Where have all the grannies gone? I mean the genuine, original, 22-carat articles, who wore black shawls and cameo brooches, sat in rocking chairs and smelled of camphor?

Keith Waterhouse

Becoming a grandmother
is great fun because you can
use the kid to get back at
your daughter.

Roseanne

The simplest toy, one which
even the youngest child can
operate, is called
a grandparent.

Sam Levenson

I was looking after my six-year-old grandson and I suggested we go into the garden to get some potatoes to cook for dinner. He was digging away when he suddenly looked at me with a very puzzled expression, and said, "Nana, why do you bury your potatoes?"

Pat Boucher

After Sunday school, my grandaughter asked thoughtfully, "Grandad, were you in the ark?" "Of course not!" I replied. "Then why weren't you drowned?"

James Potter

As a child, I went into the study of my grandfather, Winston Churchill. "Grandpapa," I said, "is it true that you are the greatest man in the world?" "Yes, now bugger off."

Nicholas Soames

— Homer, are you really
going to ignore your father
for the rest of your life?
— Of course not, Marge, just
for the rest of his life.

**Marge and Homer Simpson,**
*The Simpsons*

I'm very proud of my gold pocket watch. My grandfather, on his deathbed, sold me this watch.

**Woody Allen**

My grandmother was a very tough woman. She buried three husbands. Two of them were just napping.

Rita Rudner

I was talking to my Nan about Ant and Dec. She didn't know which one Dec was. I said, "Do you know which one Ant is?" She said, "Yes."

Jimmy Carr

Oh, Grannie, you shouldn't be carrying all those groceries! Next time, make two trips.

Nathan Lane

A glass of wine with lunch?
Is that wise? You know you
have to reign all afternoon.

The Queen Mother
to Queen Elizabeth II

— Who do you think
you are?
— Mummy, the Queen.

The Queen Mother and
Queen Elizabeth II

My parents did a really scary thing recently. They bought a caravan. This means that they can pull up in front of my house anytime now and just live there.

Paula Poundstone

— It seems like only yesterday that Dad moved in with you.

— Isn't it interesting that two people can have completely opposite impressions of the same event.

Niles and Frasier Crane, *Frasier*

My parents live in a retirement community, which is basically a minimum-security prison with a golf course.

Joel Warshaw

No matter how old a mother is, she watches her middle-aged children for signs of improvement.

Florida Scott-Maxwell

The denunciation of the young is a necessary part of the hygiene of older people and greatly assists the circulation of their blood.

Logan Pearsall Smith

The reason people blame
things on the previous
generation is that there's only
one other choice.

Doug Larson

Your kids will forgive you someday. Of course, by then you'll be dead.

Sophia Petrillo, *The Golden Girls*

Always be nice to your children, because they are the ones who will choose your rest home.

**Phyllis Diller**

Retirement homes are great. It's like being a baby, only you're old enough to appreciate it.

Homer Simpson, *The Simpsons*

I could smell the funny odour rest homes always seem to have: a mixture of roast lamb, chloroform and little jobs.

Dame Edna Everage

I have been asked to pose for *Penthouse* on my hundredth birthday. Everybody is going to be sorry.

Dolly Parton

I don't want to live to be a hundred. I don't think I could stand to see bellbottom trousers three times.

Jeff Foxworthy

— To what do you attribute
your long life?
— To the fact that I haven't
died yet.

Interviewer and Sir Malcolm Sargent

My grandmother just passed away. She was 104 years old. I went to buy some flowers and the guy there says, "Ooh, 104? How'd she die?" *How'd she die?* She was 104! I told him, "Well, it's all right – they saved the baby."

Larry the Cable Guy

If you live to be 90 in England and can still eat a boiled egg, they think you deserve the Nobel Prize.

Alan Bennett

— You've reached the ripe old age of 121. What do you expect the future will be like?
— Very short.

Interviewer and Jeanne Calment

Hugh Hefner now has seven girlfriends – one for each day of the week. Someone needs to tell him that those are nurses.

Jay Leno

I wouldn't be caught dead marrying a woman old enough to be my wife.

Tony Curtis

Age does not protect
you from love. But love,
to some extent, protects you
from age.

Jeanne Moreau

Your place or back to the sheltered accommodation?

Barry Cryer

The advantages of dating younger men is that on them everything, like hair and teeth, is in the right place as opposed to being on the bedside table or bathroom floor.

Candace Bushnell

Trouble is, by the time you
can read a girl like
a book, your library card
has expired.

Milton Berle

I want to be married to my wife until we forget each other's names. My wife is the only one who knows what I used to be, and she is starting to lose a little of it too, so we are breaking down in tandem.

Bill Cosby

When people ask me, sotto voce, in surprise, "So what about the age difference between you and your husband, Percy?" I usually shrug, smile and quip, "So, if he dies, he dies."

Joan Collins

Now that I'm 78, I do tantric sex because it's very slow. My favourite position is called the plumber. You stay in all day, but nobody comes.

John Mortimer

Pass me my teeth
and I'll bite you.

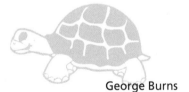

George Burns

I can still enjoy sex at 75. I live at 76, so it's no distance.

Bob Monkhouse

A little old lady in the nursing home holds up her clenched fist and announces, "Anyone who can guess what I have in my closed hand can have sex with me tonight." An elderly gentleman calls out, "An elephant." "Close enough," she replies.

Anon

I'm at the stage of life
when I'd give up a night of
wild rapture with Denzel
Washington for a nice report
on my next bone density test.

**Judith Viorst**

If it weren't for speed bumps, pickpockets and frisking at airports, I'd have no sex life at all.

Rodney Dangerfield

If it wasn't for the rectal probe I'd have no sex life at all.

Barry Cryer

We spend our lives on the run. We get up by the clock, eat and sleep by the clock, get up again, go to work, and then we retire. And what do they give us? A bloody clock.

Dave Allen

I'm taking early retirement.
I want my share of Social
Security before the whole
system goes bust.

David Letterman

My husband has just retired.
I married him for better or
for worse, but not for lunch.

Hazel Weiss

As I get older the years just
fly by. I don't think there was
an April this year.

**Jeremy Hardy**

When one subtracts from life infancy (which is vegetation), sleep, eating and swilling, buttoning and unbuttoning – how much remains of downright existence? The summer of a dormouse.

Lord Bryon

If you were going to die soon and had only one phone call you could make, who would you call and what would you say? And why are you waiting?

Stephen Levine

For every person who has
ever lived there has come, at
last, a spring he will never
see. Glory then in the springs
that are yours.

Pam Brown

I don't want to get to the end
of my life and find that I lived
just the length of it. I want
to have lived the width of it
as well.

Diane Ackerman

It's never too late to be what
you might have been.

George Eliot

You're never too old. A person of 60 can grow as much as a child of six. Michelangelo did some of his best paintings when past 80; George Bernard Shaw was still writing plays at 90; Grandma Moses didn't even begin painting until she was 79.

Maxwell Naltz

Don't save things "for best".
Drink that vintage bottle of wine
– from your best crystal glasses.
Wear your best designer jacket
to go down to the post office to
collect your pension. And, every
morning, spritz yourself with that
perfume you save for parties.

Geraldine Mayer

Don't ever save anything for a special occasion. Being alive is the special occasion.

Avril Sloe

Let's not go out and get denture cream. Let's go to the nude beach and let our wrinkled selves hang out! We'll sit on the boardwalk and watch the old men rearrange themselves when they come out of the water.

Sophia Petrillo, *The Golden Girls*

I believe you should live each day as if it was your last, which is why I don't have any clean laundry, because who wants to wash clothes on the last day of their life?

Jack Handey

Enjoying sex, loving fashion, having fun, decorating our homes, going on lavish holidays – the list is endless. Onward!

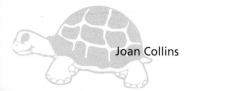

Joan Collins

What is wrong with settling down with a good book into a rocking chair by the fireside, wearing a comfy pair of slippers, if that is what makes you happy?

Eloise Pagett

As life goes on, don't you find
that all you need is about two
real friends, a regular supply
of books, and a Peke?

P. G. Wodehouse

The members seated in the Pavilion at the Test Match declined to join in the Mexican Wave. Well, when you get to a certain age, every time you just get out of you chair, it's a bit of an adventure.

Henry Blofeld

Old age isn't so bad when
you consider the alternative.

Maurice Chevalier

Like everyone else who makes
the mistake of getting older,
I begin each day with coffee
and obituaries.

Bill Cosby

# How young can you die of old age?

Steven Wright

Where would I like my ashes
scattered? I don't know.
Surprise me.

Bob Hope

I told my wife I want to be cremated. She's planning a barbecue.

Rodney Dangerfield

They say such lovely things
about people at their funerals,
it's a shame I'm going to miss
mine by just a few days.

Bob Monkhouse

There's nothing like a morning funeral for sharpening the appetite for lunch.

Arthur Marshall

When I approach the pearly gates, I'd like to hear a champagne cork popping, an orchestra tuning up and the sound of my mother laughing.

Patricia Routledge

Life is a great surprise. I do not see why death should not be an even greater one.

Vladimir Nabokov

Old age is like waiting in the departure lounge of life. Fortunately, we are in England and the train is bound to be late.

Milton Shulman

Live well, learn plenty, laugh often, love much.

Ralph Waldo Emerson